DATE DUE

FEB 22 2017	
MAY 17 2017	
AUG 10 2017	
JAN 29 2020	
DEC 11 2021	
OCT 10 2022	

The Moon

by Martha E. H. Rustad

CAPSTONE PRESS
a capstone imprint

Little Pebble is published by Capstone Press,
1710 Roe Crest Drive, North Mankato, Minnesota 56003
www.capstonepub.com

Library of Congress Cataloging-in-Publication Data
Rustad, Martha E. H. (Martha Elizabeth Hillman), 1975– author.
The moon / by Martha E. H. Rustad.
pages cm. — (Little pebble. Space)
Audience: Ages 5–7.
Audience: K to grade 3.
Summary: "Simple text and full-color photographs describe the Moon"—Provided by the publisher.
Includes bibliographical references and index.
ISBN 978-1-4914-8323-7 (library binding)
ISBN 978-1-4914-8327-5 (paperback)
ISBN 978-1-4914-8331-2 (eBook PDF)
1. Moon—Juvenile literature. I. Title.
QB582.R87 2016
523.3—dc23 2015023309

Editorial Credits
Erika L. Shores, editor; Juliette Peters and Katelin Plekkenpol, designers; Tracy Cummins, media researcher; Katy LaVigne, production specialist

Photo Credits
Science Source: Gary Hincks, 7; Shutterstock: Aphelleon, 15, godrick, cover, 1, Kalenik Hanna, Design Element, Keith Publicover, 9, Sarun T, 21, Suppakij1017, 5, Tom Reichner, 18-19, 19 right, Tristan3D, 11, Wikimedia: Jay Tanner, 17, NASA, 13

Editor's Note
In this book's photographs, the sizes of objects and the distances between them are not to scale.

Printed and bound in China.
007475LEOS16

Table of Contents

In the Sky

A full moon shines.

It glows at night.

What is the moon?

It is a big round rock!

A moon orbits a planet.

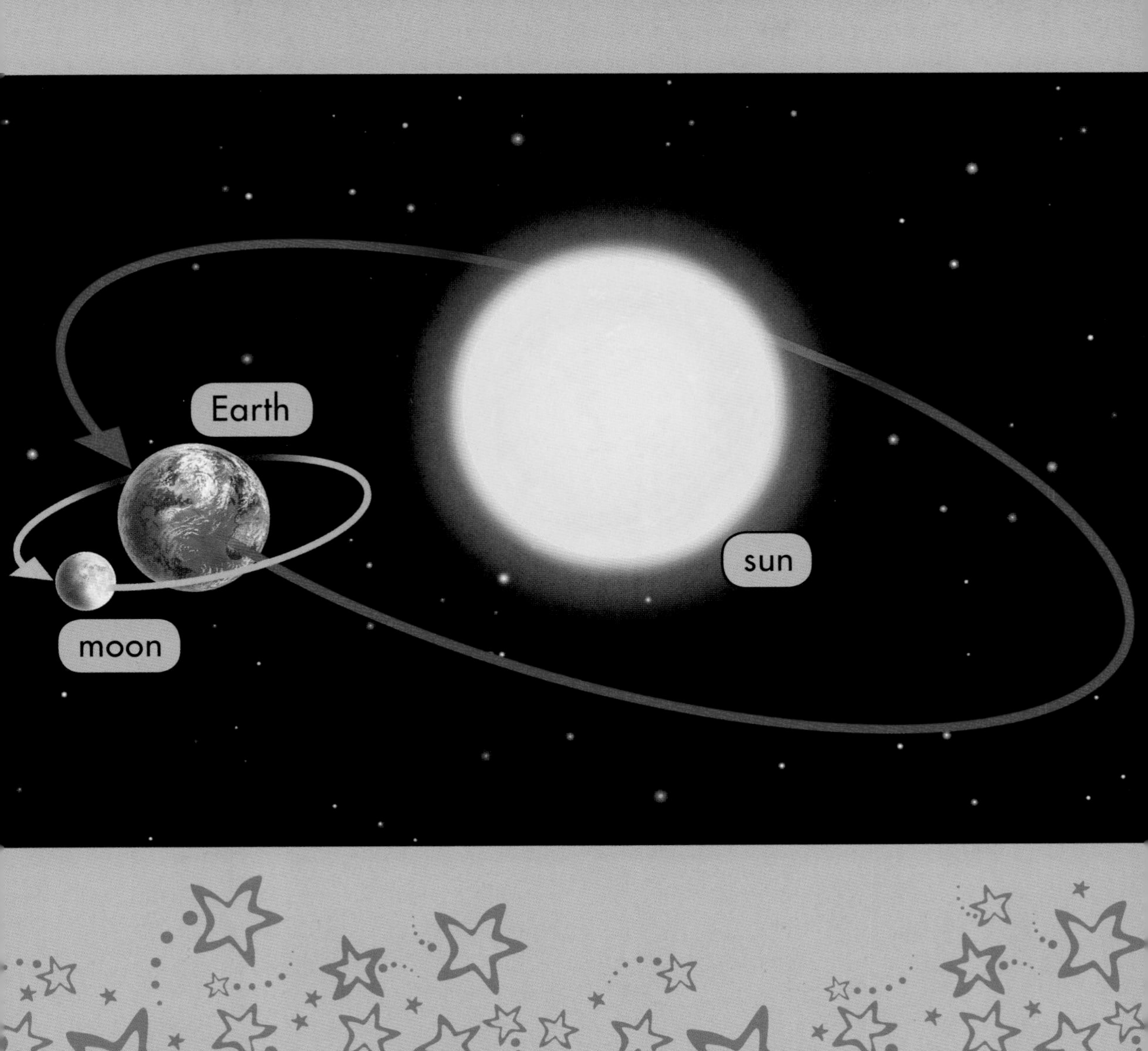
Earth
sun
moon

The moon is 239,000 miles
(384,600 kilometers)
away from Earth.
What if we could drive there?
It would take 153 days!

A Big Rock

The moon is 2,160 miles (3,476 km) wide.

Four moons could fit inside Earth.

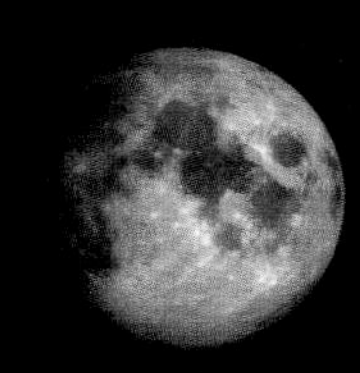

MOON

EARTH

Dust covers the moon.

It has craters all over it.

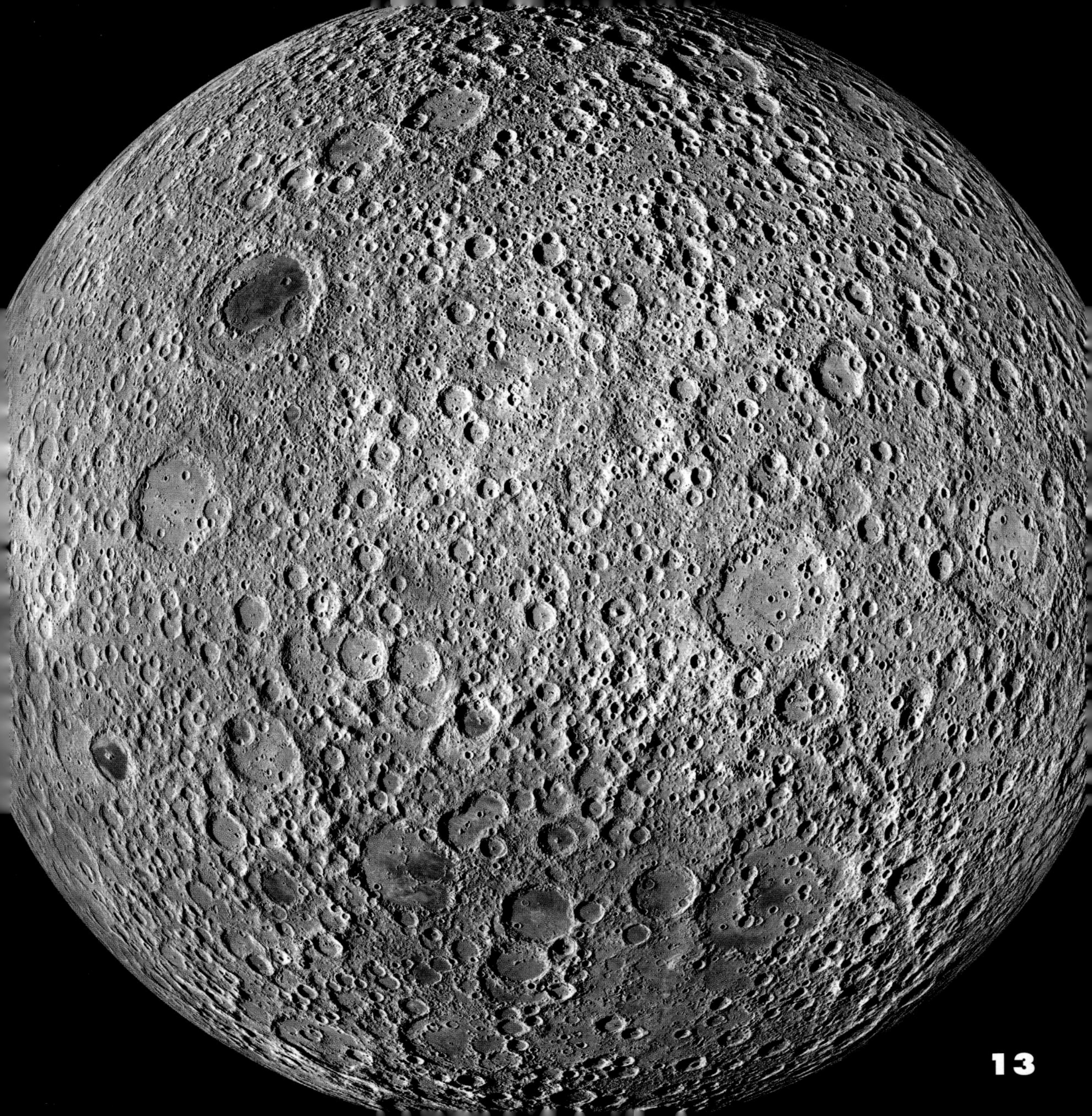

The Moon and Earth

Sunlight hits the moon. The light bounces back to Earth.

Half of the moon is
very hot.
Half is very cold.

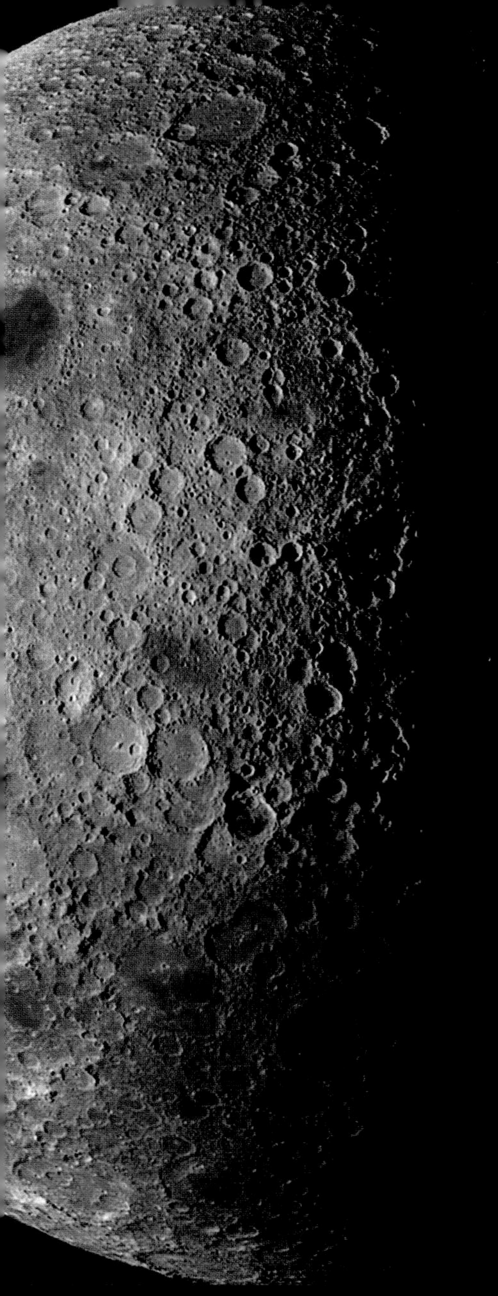

How much of the moon
do we see?
It is always changing.
Look! A full moon.
Look! A sliver moon.

Earth needs the moon.

It pulls ocean tides.

Thank you, moon!

Glossary

crater—a large, bowl-shaped hole

orbit—to follow a curved path around an object in space

planet—a large object in space that orbits a star

tide—the rising and falling of ocean water; tides move twice each day

Read More

Beaton, Kathryn. *The Moon Changes Shape.* Tell Me Why. Ann Arbor, Mich.: Cherry Lake Publishing, 2015.

DeYoe, Aaron. *Moons.* Out of this World. Minneapolis: Abdo Publishing, 2016.

Graham, Ian. *Our Moon.* Space. Mankato, Minn.: Smart Apple Media, 2015.

Internet Sites

FactHound offers a safe, fun way to find Internet sites related to this book. All of the sites on FactHound have been researched by our staff.

Here's all you do:
Visit *www.facthound.com*
Type in this code: 9781491483237

Check out projects, games and lots more at
www.capstonekids.com

Index